LETTERS from the JUNTA

LETTERS from the JUNTA
Ezekiel Black

Spuyten Duyvil
New York City

Copyright © 2019 by Ezekiel Black
ISBN 978-1-949966-24-4
All rights reserved

Cover Art: Stanley Bermudez, *Fidel Castro*, 30" × 24"
acrylic on canvas
Cover Design: Ezekiel Black
Book Design: Ezekiel Black

Library of Congress Cataloging-in-Publication Data

Names: Black, Ezekiel, author.
Title: Letters from the Junta / Ezekiel Black.
Description: New York City : Spuyten Duyvil, [2019]
Identifiers: LCCN 2019006320 | ISBN 9781949966244
Classification: LCC PS3602.L276 A6 2019 | DDC 811/.6--dc23
LC record available at https://lccn.loc.gov/2019006320

for Jordan and Zelda

Contents

The Uncertain Trumpet	1
—Push	3
Some Honesty	4
i ate Of Change	6
r_ive	7
On Benefits	9
ham	11
eat	13
A Classic	16
water, the oceans	18
Yellow	20
Security Force	22
to Help	24
Rooted	25
Chief of Coffins	26
man Looking Away	28
Judges	29
Book of Guerrillas	31
Zookeepers Wary of Virus	33
Ex- Sentence	35
WINE	37
Condo by Picasso:	39
Found War	40
CORRECTIONS	42
NEW	43
BUSINESS DAY	44
HE_ARTS	45
ION	46

mark	47
CHRIST	49
Skills Test	51
lest	52
Exit	54
Diagnal [*sic*]	56
By George	57
I Worked	59
ill Plant	60
Y	62
Sweep Away	64
Look:	66
THE MINIMALIST	68
Acknowledgments	70
Biographical Notes	72

The Uncertain Trumpet

O

sacrifice
the

broken
bed

O offer
the question
that

lays [*sic*]
in

the grain
there, rot is

the

burden
borne by
an ax

O
to save

even the
down

is
sin
I

bestride ash like a co-
lossus.

I

a_m

omnibus

This
per-
verse
b
e
d

did

muddle

the Old Order

I

blow the trumpet

–Push

WASHINGTON—
"once in a generation"

reflects his

own reshaping

He would
arrest

the

maelstrom

of farmers
and

trim
the farm

He would shrink

from

that [which]
some
consider overly
rosy.

Some Honesty

President
Washington [was]
blind   :   George_'s
axe

cut more than
that Bush
A pledge is imperative.
Without it,
louts
could lose faith in the
dol-
lar
Control is
necessary to sustain the economy—when it comes.

O the folly of unconstrained knowledge

But

one
par_t

doesn't

burden us

He

was
the first President

from

'bama

i ate Of Change

consequences

break the
icy

thing like a noun
on Thursday

The
rats
of
depression
pass

the bank disappointing.
fears
bud

around the edges

for a
hat's not enough to
cover

the

heart

r_ive

will

red ink

bubble

in a
quagmire

swollen

as a
rat? ink

reflected

on
the
remains?
A
rat

this

d_e_a_d

tells us
more

lurk over that horizon: sooner or
later we're going to have to

find
t
h
e
m

. There's only
ink
in the midst
, for now.

On Benefits

a

dollar

is a
rank

bill

and

The Republic of
Alabama

protests

i_t_s

issue.
For

Mr. September who

is

not

able to draw
his wife
dollars
make

a person

fe_ral

. Such

People

***States weigh
the unemployed.***

---

might
be
unreasonable,

willing to sacrifice the
lives of so many Texans

ham

if

a neighbor

is a
battle

The noun

ham

is like an airstrike
, and the
commitment

drones

foreign

in the

commit-
ted

The

ex-
change

had
been frank
, if somewhat general.
The next meeting
will

involve

a tense dinner

during which the
guest

s_a_y_s

"I found the North Koreans

eat

lead
and
sing for

crisis once again.
A

savage
people

in

visions
come

and ª rope

called a
tent dangerous

Mr. L

was
found

in
the

backyard

last time

Mr. L said
the host was not strong

in the

arms.

Mr.

S

expressed
t
h
a
t

i
f

this

lead

were to

storm

the liver
a new constitution
could

be devised

Mr. D

warned
that "nobody should play around
with Rupublika."

A Classic

Here's a
story—
a
story
, to be exact,

, of course,
for
teenagers

tha_t

updates, namely

,

after all, the Shakespearean
tragedy of love undone by
th_e reds

recalling
an Honest

picture of

1950s garb

—right
down to the
brass buttons.

water, the oceans

So

in a single day the
diver

turned into gas

A
grandmother remembers the
man 'round 60
years ago
tanning The
end no one

s_a_w

here's the problem:
most divers

alarm

Cuba

now,

on^l y

footprints

exist
crippling

light
cast

on to a rug

Yellow

the

millen-
nium rising

w_e sew the
seas in great quantity, these
times

counting, according
, according

the nutrient
water

And

sew w_e
d_o,

taxing
the century
, but
people
must serve more than ice
When
lions of
the

harbor

charge
beaches

break

aquatic

Security Force

training

a
roach

to

train

a
bee

to

train

a
seal

to

ply
the

sea

keeps
the

cobra
with

the hawk
, who spent his
life in uni-
form
, when
the

roach

understands the need for
a

homeland. We have
come to accept that.

to Help

It's been clear for months

—until this week,
when
c_a_m_e
the riders.

The plan is

to
pay
a

tribute.
8 percent.

That part of the
proposal has caused the most controversy
Many argue that such reward

would
but set them
to

kill the city's
dismantled

Rooted

a graveyard

to

new
men

matter is

muted

The fi-
nite [are] not

to dwell on

mass

Indeed, the

town

storm_s
the
cemetery

naked—with only two small pairs of
eyeglasses on

Chief of Coffins

—I

in

coffins

lie
a
s

a
blanket on a

chief

I think
about
giving
a
news conference
Renewed
by the

privacy and dignity
of the dead

I

demur
But

I'll be perfectly honest,
a division

from the

dead
is a

conclusion that we should not
presume
; we should
let them

lace

the
swift

What is the
casket
other than

a can to

cook hot dogs in

man Looking Away

—The

thighbone jutting out of

a

Knight

was
the territory of Poland

men, women and children
inhabit
the city along

the
wou[n]d
all
skulls have bullet holes

nowhere is
that more true than in Germany

Judges

I the author
people the

swamp

with judges, and they are
numb

. In addition, the flood of

many debtors will [not] disap-
point.
Debtors will argue
,
will win
these contests: they
have more expertise in
their

uncertainty. A
crisis is
their

neighborhood and a
house is

But
a house
, and thus

judges

will likely be
shot in the dark,

Book of Guerrillas

the

heroine

is a fish

"I want
her

savage"
said

the au-
thor

"infected
with the jungle,"

Indeed,

the book

is her captor

,
plucked

o
u
t

he-
r eye.
The book is

a

squirrel
throwing a fit about
the color of a mattress
(It was baby blue.)
.

Zookeepers Wary of Virus

Zookeepers
feared the

slug

was
a deadly
virus
A
laboratory
analysis

said

"It's such a mystery-
ous disease, and it has n
                o
                    t a symptom."

Still,

bubble-gum
pale and speckled

was
the vi-
rus.

American zoos

working with available
samples

know lit-
tle about the disease, including
how it is transmitted. Nor can
they say

why certain strains die
and others don't.

The virus exists in captive and
wild populations
, and

"There are big outbreaks
where you'll see whole herds of
the
virus,"

Ex- Sentence

A former

sen-
tence

pleaded
guilty to mail fraud for the sale
of a state owned

yak

and

was
barred from

the college's library, his home country. A spokeswoman
said the

yak

taught on campus

. The

sentence
acted

a
s

i
f

a Specter

WINE

I

am

"poor," but

eye the

port
I
am a
text

her imp
like

influ-
ence

marks

me
word for word

—

its

ill

widespread

arms

hand

me

a rose

Condo by Picasso:

Picasso , Warhol
and Dali

ate

insurance

Found War

PARIS
is
n_o

strongman

o o o. But

b_y

judging
[de] Milo
o o o,

he

led
to a nearly three-month bombing

o o o
bombing

bombing of a

television

, and
he

stood
on

the refu-

se to

exer-
cise

o o o
, which made

de
Milo

sp_-

end

Thursday

in

o o o

hiding

CORRECTIONS

art about
people
scattershot

in

a restaurant
ministers
to blood-
sugar levels

; the
pump itself is not inserted un-
der the skin.

NEW

art
about
a man and
his hat

is, at one point,
the name of a treaty

a mechanism to
child abduction
. As noted elsewhere, it is
Abduction—
Adoption—Convention.

BUSINESS DAY

art
about the quarterly
isat [stet]
the source a comment

on Macy's. un
quote

HE_ARTS

art
about
a field will hit
hard

organ by

organ. It is the
Prototype,
Prototype

this
art
is
the

face

of
misidenti-
fied Acupunc-
ture

ION

art about

theft is
one of
error
It was

Paul
—who said: "The

years
numb
the air

a
column on
decline

that drop

—fell in the last half of

Wednesday

mark

A bishop

on Thursday

denied the existence of
gas
he

said, "I
can say that
such

rise

would have made them
all souls

."

he said that no

gas

needs docu-
mentation

a
television

was

pope
s_o

the Vatican

sent

for

Jésus

CHRIST

I was

A mixture of vegetables

spin-
ach made from

was I

A few weeks ago

I
called

upon a black "dirt"

it evolved

He wanted

a mirror

He said he was
the dirt

i

credit
his creation to

the land around the res-
taurant.

·Skills Test

I ate

his
stamp and
left
him

the rice

, and,
a good
flood-
gate, his
anger could

trouble
almost any

demon
from

Oklahoma

, "much
as he did in 1932 and 1980."

lest

They eat air—
where

Rows of Land

read

Redemption."
this

desert guards
men [who]
took meals on their laps.

it
is real

they have
complete confidence in

the new

no one
doubts

[that]

Some have been

taken
t_o

a
world called

elsewhere

Exit

the way
in Decem-
ber
is

mercury poisoning.

hear the
star

tear
that
orient

a grievance

against
January.

hear

all

who reflect
The
end

they

rule

a more rigorous

home

on medication

Diagnal [*sic*]

The problems are

a system

A system
means

access to
paper

the
new
drug_s

comprise
a Deep well

our

families store and track
medical devices

The

French

Monitor elderly patients in their homes,

By George

I, an apple
be-
longing to a
school teacher and his
wife, wasn't
exceptional—

I was di-
vided in two:

The liquids and solids

the couple
so delighted
after all.
What does this have to do with you?

the dust of
those who
waste me
c_ements the
great
house-
holds
I

a_m
n_o
cholera

I Worked

I
took a
job in the

future
The

trouble
has been the subject of tense   for
talks

express—ed [that] a

peach

in a
pond
a_m

I

ill Plant

I
sit at
a window
cele-
brating another

plant
displaced

The sale of what had been

the greening of
the weath-
er

w_a_s

a grift

Win-
dows like
a father who lost his
January, the
prospect
was "a dream come true."

Hav-
ing another

Red
Oak

shuttered

represents a

great
hope for
me
, a

bitter

house

plant.

Y

cut
the grain

bucolic,
for

Thursday
unveiled a

promenade

The city plans to

[b]loom the

stoop.
People avoid

people

overlooking

"People
stuck in traffic,"

the ex-
citement

of
passionate reactions, of
driven
self-interest:

"I like the happy hubbub," said

the
sidewalks

Sweep Away

to
end the era
dominated by

tables—a bold,
even radical depar-
ture from

formality and stasis
—would
reduce

the rich
to
lint

They

use the middle-class
like
s_o

much
ice

Mr. police[man]
is
already
eating
a
l_E_g

Look:

a
couple
lost
weight

all in the name of

fish.
their children

cut back on
alcohol. Whatever they did,

the losers are
the champions

Mr.
Avant-Garde himself

does not look like the same per-
son.
And

through a
program of drinks
and moderate lunches
he was muscle

We have seen
power in
recent years,

[but]

"You have to be a little skeptic-

THE MINIMALIST

EVEN
The fears: never rise
they're temperamental.
A soufflé is a
soufflé

bitten
on Valentine's Day.

your significant other
i_s

a mixture of flour and fat

Do not cheat

sh_e

i_s

ready to bake.
cover
her with plastic wrap

and

stand in the kitchen

Acknowledgments

I would like to thank these journals for publishing my poetry:

Fjords — to Help / water, the oceans / Found War / Security Force

Denver Quarterly — Look: / mark / Book of Guerrillas / Exit

Grand Central Review — man Looking Away / On Benefits / ill Plant

inter|rupture — Chief of Coffins

Backlash Press — The Uncertain Trumpet / A Classic / Ham

BOAAT Press — Sweep Away / r_ive

iO: A Journal of New American Poetry — Judges / i ate of Change

Glitterpony

THE MINIMALIST
CHRIST
Diagnal [*sic*]
—Push

Biographical Notes

EZEKIEL BLACK is a Senior Lecturer of English at The University of North Georgia and edits the audio journal for experimental poetry *Pismire* (pismirepoetry.org). He attended  the University of Massachusetts Amherst, where he received an MFA in Creative Writing. His poetry and reviews have appeared in *Verse, Sonora Review, Tarpaulin Sky, Drunken Boat, CutBank, Columbia: A Journal of Literature and Art, BOAAT Press, inter|rupture, Denver Quarterly, Fjords,* and elsewhere. He lives in Greater Atlanta with his wife and daughter.

STANLEY BERMUDEZ is a visual artist currently living and working in Athens, Georgia. Bermudez was born in New Orleans but was raised in Maracaibo, Venezuela. In 1990, he received a BFA from Sam Huston State University, Texas, and in 2000, he received an MFA from Radford University, Virginia. Since 1990, Bermudez has been concentrating on painting. Fidel Castro's portrait is part of the Continuity series, a set of Pop-art/Op-art portraits of members of his family, people in American and Latin American history, and people in American and Venezuelan popular culture. Bermudez works with acrylics on canvas, using a hard edge approach that does not blend any colors. Bermudez's use of vibrant colors comes from his childhood in Venezuela.

www.ingramcontent.com/pod-product-compliance
Lightning Source LLC
Chambersburg PA
CBHW020121130526
44591CB00031B/240